To Rodney.
From Love mom
1960

'TO A VERY SPECIAL'® AND 'TO-GIVE-AND-TO-KEEP'® ARE
REGISTERED TRADE MARKS OF EXLEY PUBLICATIONS LTD AND
EXLEY GIFTBOOKS.

Other mini books in this series:

To a very Special Dad	To a very Special Daughter
To a very Special Friend	To my very Special Husband
To a very Special Grandmother	Merry Christmas
To a very Special Mother	Happy Anniversary
To my very Special Love	To a very Special Granddaughter
To my very Special Wife	Wishing You Happiness

To our own very special sons
  Lincoln and Dalton
  and Colin
To say the things they won't allow us to say out loud.

Published simultaneously in 1993 by Exley Publications Ltd in Great
Britain, and Exley Giftbooks in the USA.

12 11 10 9 8 7

© Helen Exley 1993.
ISBN 1-85015-424-4
A copy of the CIP data is available from the British Library on request.
Edited by Helen Exley.
Typeset by Delta, Watford.
Designed by Pinpoint Design Company.
Printed and bound in Hungary.

**Exley Publications Ltd., 16 Chalk Hill, Watford, Herts WD1 4BN,
United Kingdom.**
Exley Giftbooks, 232 Madison Avenue, Suite 1206, NY 10016, USA.

To a very special
SON

Written by Pam Brown
Illustrations by Juliette Clarke

I must not dream dreams for you.
Only give you the chance to dream
your own – and do all I can to
help you make them come true.

. . .

≣EXLEY
NEW YORK • WATFORD, UK

Every mother cries silently to her sons – be bold, be brave – but be very, very, careful!

. . .

A SON IS...

– the one who believes that if it's in the refrigerator it's there to be eaten.

– someone who regards you as an amiable idiot – but loves you all the same.

– the one who regards you as the totally reliable source of clean shirts.

– the indignant one who wants to do things for you. It's just getting round to it.

– the guy who flings himself. He bounces, bumps,
ducks, dives, slides, pounds, paddles, fidgets
– and falls. Then he picks himself up and does
it all again.

- the one who cheerfully lets himself in at 3:00 a.m.
– all set to tell you what a wonderful time he's
had. And is hurt and astounded to find you don't
want to know.

the softie who gives you a gorgeous gift in a brown
paper bag, with the price still on it.

- the voice who reverses the telephone charges from
Bangkok and says he knows you will not mind.
(Which, of course, you don't.)

– the bloke pulling his motorbike apart in the
kitchen because it's raining.

– the fellow with all the friends that you find
sleeping on the living room floor.

– the boy who says things that drive his parents to
the edge – but smiles at exactly the right moment.

HAPPINESS IS A SON

Sons teach you how to laugh again.

Loudly.

. . .

When nothing's gone right all day and you're feeling
the weight of every failure, it only needs the rush of
small feet pounding down the path, a leap, arms
locked about you, a grin, a pouring out of the day's
news – and everything goes your way.

. . .

I think I must have done something special in my
life to deserve a son like you.

. . .

Even if a son is in and out of the house in ten
minutes flat, he leaves behind him a great swirl
of fresh air.

. . .

However hard the day has been, the smiling face of a
small son pressed against a window pane is a
sure-fire remedy.

. . .

Parents don't know perfect happiness until
they've swung their small child high in the air –
shouting with joy!

. . .

A son is the biggest bonus life can offer.

. . .

THANK YOU FOR EVERYTHING

Thank you for putting exclamation marks in my life

. . .

Thank you for the cups of cold tea when you were
very small ("I found it in the pot"). Thank you for
the fluff-covered toffees donated from your pocket.
Thank you for the peppermint-tasting kisses. Thank
you for the dead mouse. Thank you for the ice-cold
cuddles in the dead of a winter's night. Thank you
for naming your hamster after me. Thank you for
love greater than I've ever deserved.

. . .

Thank you for all your gifts – all your kindnesses.
Like the dead frog and the wilting dandelions and
the mud puddings.
Like the tie-dye scarf and the clay elephant and the
drawing of Tiger-cat.
Like the pond you dug, lined, filled and planted
when I'd been lured to friends for the day.
All of them treasured still.

. . .

Thank you for never, *never* buying me bubble bath.
Or scarves. Or cyclamen.
Thank you for giving me a delivery of horse manure
– well-rotted down. And wild-bird peanuts.

. . .

Son – thank you for getting under my feet, causing
me sleepless nights, costing me a small fortune,
interfering with my plans. What on earth would I
have done with my time without you?

. . .

GROWING PAINS

Small sons should be patented as dirt collectors.
It is a proven fact that paint, glue, mud, soot, oil,
ink, jam, scum and ketchup will leap considerable
distances to adhere to them. The difficulty is
removing the dirt from the dirt collectors. No soap
or scourer has yet been invented that will
completely clean a small son. Thankfully, the grime
wears off with the passage of years.

. . .

A head comes round the door. A worried face. A staccato of blown kisses. What has he dropped? What has he smashed? What has he torn?

"It's all right, Love. It can't be as bad as that. Come and tell me." He has the pieces in his hand.

"I didn't ackcherly do it. It sort of slipped. And there it was. Broke. I'm *sorry*."

Ah well. Boys are more precious than possessions.

. . .

Sons, as they grow older, are inclined to be horribly embarrassed by their parents. Forgetting the times they went berserk in museums, retreated under the table in restaurants, shouted during solemn ceremonies, vomited on grandma's new carpet....

. . .

Almost all sons go through a Bad Patch, when their parents would cheerfully trade them in for a twenty-year-old Ford. Thankfully, they usually come out of it just before the deal is struck.

. . .

Everyone should have a son...

to give them a cheerful grin when the world is drab.

to praise their cooking when it's not that wonderful.

to give them unexpected hugs.

to bring home surprises – frogs, engine parts,

girlfriends with green hair.

to lure them into adventures ("You'll *love* it, Dad.

Pull the ripcord and there you are...").

to widen their minds ("OK – so it's Hard Rock.

Just let the music sink into your *bones*.")

to increase their circle of friends (This is Bob,

Ma. He's a Flat-Earther.")

to stimulate their brains ("But I have to know by

tomorrow, in detail, what was Mithraism?")

to sharpen their vocabulary ("Do that just once

more, Son, and I'll....)

to teach them patience ("I'll do it later, I swear I

will. After I've done this.")

to love.

. . .

PROUD OF YOU

"My son" – the happiest introduction.

. . .

A mother's proudest boast of any of her sons is not his wealth or his success – but that he is a good son, a good friend. A decent person.

. . .

Parents glow a little when people say "Isn't he handsome? Isn't he charming? Hasn't he done well?" But they treasure forever "Isn't he kind?, "He always remembers...", "I'd trust him with my life."

. . .

I am very proud of you – not so much for your achievements, but for staying sane and kind and caring in a world where such things seem less important than projecting the Right Image. Whatever your position you will have succeeded. For you'll not be spoken of with awe or fear or envy – but with affection and with respect.

. . .

Parents are very proud if they produce geniuses. But rather relieved if they don't.

. . .

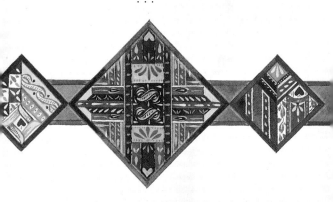

I wish I could ensure you good health, lasting
friendships, true love, satisfying work, just
recognition, adventures enough to keep your
mind and heart alive. I'd get it all down in
writing, have it witnessed.

But I can't. No parent can.

All we can do is hope – and always be
here for you.

. . .

What do I wish you? Strength. Not necessarily
of body - but of mind and heart. Strength to
endure when hope has dwindled,
when those you
thought believed in you have turned away,
when love has failed.

. . .

I wish you a mind that never ceases to learn and to wonder.

. . .

I wish for you, dear son, enough changes in your life and thought to keep life fresh and new until its very end.

. . .

I wish you love, friendships with both human beings and so-called lesser creatures, the gift of empathy, discipline of mind, joy in the mastery of some skill and boundless curiosity. I also wish you that rare ability to forgive...yourself, as well as others.

. . .

MISSING YOU

Sons occupy far more space than
their size would indicate.
That's why the house feels so empty
when they are gone.

. . .

The TV play is reaching its climax.
The telephone rings. Cursing
inwardly, you reach for the phone.
It's your son.
So who cares about who
did the murder?

. . .

Sons flash their headlights when
they leave.
It means a lot to the shadow
standing
at the window.

. . .

f parents are over-given to warnings and anxieties,
it's because age has given them the high ground –
and they can see where the flowery paths are
ading. They care too much about you to keep their
mouths shut.

. . .

There comes a time when the toys are all packed
away up in the attic, when the door opens on
to neatly-ordered shelves, when the laundry
basket is almost empty, when the refrigerator is full.
When one no longer has to step over books and
bikes and legs.
And that's the time a parent needs a phone call.

. . .

I have a little addendum to my list of hopes for
you. It's one for me. However wise and successful
and happy you become – send me a letter
now and then.

. . .

HOME AGAIN

A son with 'flu heads home.

. . .

There is a special smile that mothers have when all
their tall, grown offspring are home together.
Utter content.

. . .

When a son has been away, how soon he fits into his old place on his return. He may not stay - but here is a renewal in the hearts of all the family. He leaves reassured. There is one place in the world where he can be accepted for himself.

. . .

Even the best son will always regard his parents' attic as an extension of his own.

. . .

Visiting sons still remember where the cakes live.

. . .

Sons go far, take on many guises. But once with the family, the uniform, the gown, the white coat is set aside. The great world knows them in their achievement. The family knows all the mistakes, all the jokes, all the adventures, all the habits and tricks and weaknesses of a lifetime. Dr. Thomas Jenkins is plain Tom at home.

. . .

WHAT I'D GIVE TO YOU...

If I could give you only one
thing I think it would have
to be courage. With it you can
face all changes, all loss, all
rejection, all failure even
loneliness – and build anew
and more strongly than before.

. . .

I wish you the gift of love. Love that
survives all trials and that strengthen
through the years.

. . .

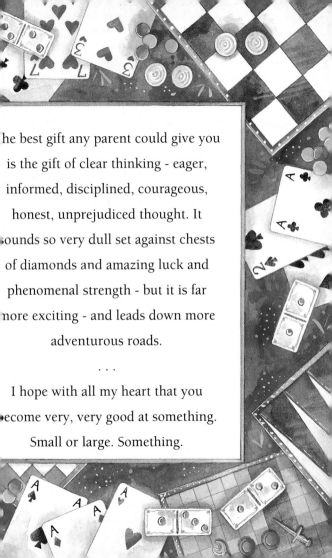

he best gift any parent could give you
is the gift of clear thinking - eager,
informed, disciplined, courageous,
honest, unprejudiced thought. It
ounds so very dull set against chests
of diamonds and amazing luck and
phenomenal strength - but it is far
nore exciting - and leads down more
adventurous roads.

. . .

I hope with all my heart that you
ecome very, very good at something.
Small or large. Something.

BONDED FOREVER

Some walk away, ride away, drive away,
sail away. They always have. But the
steel-strong, web-fine links that bind
them to those who love them and
whom they love in turn, cannot be
broken. Ever.

. . .

There is a comfortable kinship between
sons and their parents.
They seem to have a mysterious
understanding – and catch each other's
eyes, and grin.

. . .

Sons are linked to home by invisible
unbreakable threads – forever.

. . .

When you were very small I told you
that there was a gold cord that held a
family together and that whatever
happened it could never snap or fray.
eparation, divorce, distance or death –
it was always there.
Though sometimes very hard to see.
t can stretch clear over any horizon to
any point in time. A lifeline, a
reassurance, when and if you need it.

. . .

GO, WITH MY LOVE

I do not know where you will go, what you will do, whom you will love. But I stand ready to applaud.

. . .

Dear Son – I like you, love you, as you are. But I hold in my heart all the sons you've been over the years – and like and love them all. I share your life and am the closer for it.

. . .

ou take my love with you to places that I will never

see, to times that I will never know.

So love survives.

. . .

Do something for me, Love.

Do all the things I never was able to.

See the places I never saw.

Discover things beyond my understanding.

. . .

We hope, Son, you never need a bolt hole.

But if you do, we're it.

. . .

Of *course* I remember when you were very small. Of

course I have stored up all the things you did and

said, and will treasure them forever.

But it is you as you are that I love. And will,

however far you go or however much you change.

For all my life.

. . .